A RAIN WASHED EARTH

A Rain Washed Earth

CARL J. NELSON

RESOURCE *Publications* • Eugene, Oregon

Resource Publications
A division of Wipf and Stock Publishers
199 W 8th Ave, Suite 3
Eugene, OR 97401

A Rain Washed Earth
By Nelson, Carl J.
Copyright©1975 by Nelson, Carl J.
ISBN 13: 978-1-62032-121-8
Publication date 3/15/2012
Previously published by Satram Publishers, 1975

ITINERARY

Bazaars	10
My old man	12
Piles afire	13
Stones	14
A neighbor's apple orchard	15
Albert Kjellson	16
Maple syrup	18
Axel Oelke	20
Anna and Neils Neilsen	21
Constance, wife of Steve Thomson	22
Storm	24
Milton Olm	27
Mother Josephine	28
A drinking cohort	29
Old Rex	33
Loads of peas	37
Hauling gravel	39
Ned	41
Jack	42
Bess	43
Richard Nordlund	47
Cutting firewood	47
Leon Nahring	49
A heifer	50
Pigs	51
The cattle buyer	53
Kittens	55
The K. K. K.	57
Frank Moore	59
Threshing	59
Haying	62
Only two years old	64
Pallbearer	64
The winter	65
A railroad engine	67
Snowbound woods	68
After evening chores	69
Bare feet	71
Return of birds	73
The Gerings	76
Halloween	76
Oscar	79
Swimming	79
Jim Leonard	80
Model T	81
The blacksmith shop	83
Our old school	84
Teachers	86
Outhouse immunity	88

Fritz Kramer	89
A small cheese factory	90
My sister	91
Rosie	96
Visions of Canadian trappers	96
Weasel	98
Rabbits	99
Woodchucks	100
The Fourth	102

A RAIN WASHED EARTH

The steepled church
with straggled gravestones,
like a watchful mother hen with chicks,
squats on a corner of the quarter section
of what was once the family farm.

And just on west
broods the house
where I was born and raised.

    At bazaars,
we played tag
and ran barefooted over grass
that covered curious mounds
or little dips
before these stones,
or perched upon a granite marker
to savour ice cream cones,
while grown-ups crowded 'round an auctioneer
presenting offerings of the faithful
for a price.

    "And here, my friends,
we have a lovely crazy quilt!
    We'll start at 15 dollars -- nothing less --
15 dollars -- who'll start with 15 dollars?
    Ah! 15 I have!
    Who'll make it 20?
15 -- 20 I have, who'll make it 25?
25?   25?   25!!!
25 I have, who'll make it 30?   30?
25 I'm bid, who'll make it 30?

    "Really, gents,
look at this needle work!
    Think of those winter nights ahead!
    It's worth three times the bid!

"25 I have, who'll make it 30?
What's that?   26?
26 I'm bid, who'll make it 28?
26 I have, who'll make it 28?
Over there! What'd you say? 26 and a half?
26½ I have, who'll make it 27?
26½ -- going at 26½ -- going -- going -- going --

Sold! To Jim over there.
You lucky fellow.
Take it away.

"And next -- what's next?
This charming apron --
just the thing to decorate your sweetie pie.
Glenn! You blushing boy! Start it off! No?
Who'll start it at a dollar? Just one dollar?
------------------------."

And so he carried on.

So this is death
and here my old man lies.

   His grave stares blankly
next the fence
that separates the graveyard from the fields
where he had driven teams and tractors.

   I remember when that field
bristled with the wreckage
from the slashing of the forests.

   We brothers
piled the stumps, the limbs and knots
in heaps as high as houses.
   And then at night
we set the piles afire.
   Flames leapt wildly --
savage, towering tongues that soared into the night --
matched by as fierce an exultation in myself.

   The fires drove the darkness back
before a lighted circle,
and on the fringes
shadows flitted
with the whiplash of the flames.
   Angry, red-eyed sparks
swirled up in hordes into the dark

each time we threw on extra stumps and limbs.

Then

stones

were left.

    Stones offered no excitement --
only strengthened backs,
finger tips worn sensitive,
scarred arms, bruised knees, and weariness.

    Smaller stones
we tossed into the wagon;
medium ones we pickaxed out,
lugged up on a wheel
and heaved
into the box.

    But boulder sized
we rolled by push and crowbar
onto a stone boat --
wooden skids with planks spiked to the top --

and skidded with the horses to a pile.

    And there in piles
they still remain.

    Now,
after sixty years of process
starting with my dad's old man,
one sees fields of timothy
that yield in rolling waves before the wind,
corn leaves
shimmering in the sunshine,
sprays of drooping oat heads
turning golden as they ripen.

    And half a mile away I see the fence
between a neighbor's apple orchard and our fields.

That barbed wire
exacted justice
on dark and plot-filled nights
by clutching at our clothes and flesh
on a hasty getaway following an apple raid --
haste accelerated by a shotgun blast
that we were sure was aimed into the air.

   And yet we took no chances
as protesting wire squeaked on posts
and clothing ripped.

   Albert Kjellson.

   He lived a half mile west of our home place,

yet we could hear him playing on his violin
on a summer's evening.

    Not long before he died at ninety one,
his daughter visited the neighborhood,
bringing him along.
    She left him in the car while she went in,
and the neighbor woman said,
"Poor man, bring him in. He's lonely, talking to himself."
    "No", his daughter said, "he's singing to himself."

    And so he was --

    His woods
stood permissively
just across the road
west from our fields;
and in the spring
I'd tap some of his maples.

    I never asked him if I could --
the idea never struck me.
    I guess that youth has trouble
understanding absentee possession
and assumes the right to anything immediately at hand.

    We picked wild raspberries there
and never asked him either.

    And once we built a cabin,
cutting down his poplar trees.
    That was our right, I guess;
no one else was using them.

    He finally saw it
and word came back to us
he thought it was a better cabin
than some that he'd seen people living in.

    Kids may need some kind of neighbor's woods
to learn what absentee possession means,

if we must.

    I'd just as soon
old Albert here
had owned the whole wide world.

    Anyway,
I tapped some of his maples,
and an elm and ash or so.

    For spouts
one cut a half inch sapling some six inches long.
    With a red hot wire
heated in a bed of coals that glowered in the stove,
one burned a hole two inches deep into one end;
and on the rest,
split the top half off;
then with the wire on the flat split end
burned a channel connecting with the hole.

    The solid end one tapped into the tree,
a notch upon the other
held the handle of a pail
into which the sap would drip.

    Augering a hole
straight into a maple tree
taxed a man's ability.
    In the turning and the twisting
of my midget-sized Herculean efforts,
a bit would sometimes break,
and operations ceased.

    At some later date
when my dad couldn't find a half inch bit,
he would cuss and storm
while I would tighten up my lips
and disappear.

    George Washington
and a cherry tree
gained immortal fame;
but maples made me conscious of my mortal nature
when my dad couldn't find his half inch bits,
and I was willing to forego the fame I would have gotten
by volunteering information.

    A dozen trees
spelled success,
and I made the rounds,
lugging pails of sap
a half a mile out of the woods.

    My mother boiled it down
in kettles on the cook stove.
    Eventually,
she complained of how it steamed the house;
asked if it would never end,
or wasn't it a lot of work
for just that little bit of syrup.

    Why just a cup of syrup
paid for all the work,
and come to think of it,
that about was all I got.

    It was process;
you only work when you make money;
if you enjoy it, why it's process;
and the yield is not important --

provided someone else will boil it down.

A serious man,
Axel Oelke,
perhaps because he limped.

I helped to raise his barn --
one of some forty men and boys.

In the morning,
only the foundation.

In the evening

there

she stands.

　　　Born of parents by the name of Habeck
too poor to raise another son,
my old man was placed with
Anna
and
Neils Neilsen.

　　　For reasons known to him alone,
he changed his name to Nelson.

　　　What's in a name?
Habeck, Neilsen, Nelson --
I'm pretty much the same, regardless.

　　　And yet these names identified a circumstance,
and were my name now Habeck,

or Neilsen,
I would now be somewhat different.

That summer Sunday afternoon
in 1924 when
Constance,
wife of Steve Thomson,
died,
we stood on our back porch
and watched black clouds boil up into the west
while steady thunder rumbled.

It passed on north.

Telephone -- tornado!

We drove on out --

an obscenely naked house foundation,
boards, glass, roofing, clothes, possessions
strewn far into the fields --
straws driven into wood,
machines turned over,
trees uprooted.

1924 -- she died.

Those black clouds --

Clouds --

Often in the morning
little clouds like colts
will frisk along with northwest winds
of cool, clear air.

But by afternoon,
they may grow

into mountain scenes
with snow white pinnacles
and ramparts bulging high into the sky.

    Thunder storms might flash and pass,
but the weather always cleared.

    Low, black, beetling eyebrows
peering over the horizon
usually meant rain.

    Sometimes early in the morning
clouds seem ragged and chaotic,
as though awaiting some creative force
to shape them for the day;
but if red in the morning
sailors take warning;
red at night
sailor's delight.

    High-flying mares'tails
predicted fair for a day or two --
then look out.

    One hot and humid afternoon
we took warning,
as darkened clouds loomed up into the west,
and nervous horses,
unhitched from the hay rack
and unharnessed,
snorted trotting out to pasture.

    Trees seemed to droop,
exhausted in the sticky heat.
    A robin call
pointed up the silence of the birds.

    Expectancy
weighed heavily on the air.

    A faint flash --
one,
    two,
        three,
            four,
                five,
                    six,
                        seven --
rumbling thunder.

    Clouds, ominously blacker,
boiled up nearer, higher, from the west
in a furious ballet.

    A chilling gust of wind
swirled dust and leaves and paper high aloft,
while an empty pail fled clanging through the yard
to lodge against the water tank.

    A sudden flash --
a whiplash crash,
boomed and bumped and rolled.
    Then rain,
and a helter skelter race for shelter.

    Rain!
    Drenching sheets!
    Cascading torrents!

    Wind bent and whipped the trees,
stripping leaves that hurtled through the air
and made them look like pitchers
winding up and hurling baseballs.

    A moving wave across the standing hay field
marked a slanting sheet of gray
that swooshed the trees
and slammed the house.

    The building shuddered,
rattling doors and window panes.

    Sheet after sheet,
swoosh after swoosh,
slam after slam.

    Sizzling flashes
tore the clouds to shreds,
as thunder crashed and boomed and rolled.

    A slackening in the fury of the wind
allowed the sound of rain --
water spluttered gustily on window panes,
water drummed the ground beneath the eaves,
rain pummelled on the walls,
gurglings everywhere.

    A lightening --

                lessening --

                        relaxing.

    Rain subsided,
so that individualized,
it dimpled pools that flooded yard and driveway,
bubbles jumping up
soon to burst or sail away.

    Now was the time
to run barefooted through the wet morass,
and when pretense of keeping dry
could be no longer sensibly upheld,
one stood spluttering beneath the eaves.

    Muddy torrents seethed through all the ditches,
carrying debris,
and also ships of board
freighted high with patted mounds of mud
for unknown ports.

    The blackness rolled on eastward;
blue showed through the grey
and when the sky had cleared,
to the east a white and bulging column
reached high into the sky.

    A martin gurgled on the wing;
bare ground already showed the trail of angle worms;

flattened grasses tensed to rise again;
a cooling wind breathed lightly
on a rain washed earth.

    Milton Olm,
only twenty.

    Killed while hunting deer.

I felt involved
since he had borrowed my dad's new gun.

The coolness of the killing
stimulated an excitement --
a communion
with raw elements of life --
a mystical experience
holding challenge,
but very little in the way of threat
since my identity still intertwined
with family and things.

The strangeness
mystifies me yet.

Mother Josephine.

She always hoped
that I'd become a minister.

I wonder if she knew

if she'd approve.

    And here,
here lies a drinking cohort of my dad's.

    If they met in town,
hard telling when they finally left
their favorite saloon.
    And in summer,
if I had come along to town
the day would drag to afternoon
as I wilted waiting in the car.
    Later, when in high school,
I often sneaked in back doorways of saloons,
so schoolmates wouldn't see me,
and urged his coming home.

    I learned to drive quite early.

    One summer
we started a garage.
    We boys began the preparation
while the old man went to town to get cement.

We would have it up in no time;
forms were quickly set, and all we needed was cement.
   Morning melted into noon;
after lunch,
we sat glumly on the forms and threw occasional stones
at this and that,
and then we wandered off;
each on a project of his own.

   He might be home by supper time,
bleary eyed and weaving,
maybe with cement and maybe not.

   My mother'd fret and stew,
avow that she would get divorced,
but when our car would finally splutter in the driveway,
her relief relaxed her face,
and reprimand trailed off.

   A slightly taunting grin enveloped his face
as he staggered to the house.
   He never answered scoldings;
if confronted he would grin,
munch a bit on food my mother saved in the warming oven
and go to bed.

   Such was the reconciliation --
his grin;
her saving food.

   And some miles away,
Clifford had his confrontation too.

   They used to live
just a half a mile away.

One evening
we walked up there to visit
and my dad
bought a calf from Clifford,
threw it round his neck,
held the struggling feet
in two tight grips
and brought it home.

   His strength incited legendary tales,
and those who got too smart, or tested him,
got stacked in monkey-piles.

   One tale
has him ride his favorite horse
right in the door of a saloon.
   "Any place
good enough for me
is good enough for Prince."

   Once
a driver at a sawmill
whacked one of his team to make it pull
but got kicked full in the chest
and lay dying.

   My dad had to pick the kicker
to unhitch and ride to town,
hell bent for election,
to summon out a doctor.

   Poetic justice
or flamboyance?

   Maybe both,
yet he assumed no affectations.
   Like
he didn't fiddle with his cigarettes.

   They dangled from his lips
while he talked, or read,

or did whatever he was doing.

    Thinned with air,
smoke curled up,
watering his eyes
and ebbing in and out his mouth.

    The ash
would grow and lengthen,
enthralling uninitiated watchers
who wondered how he'd make the ashtray
without it breaking off and falling.

    When the ash began to bend,
facination deepened into consternation.

    Suddenly
he pursed his lips

and blew,

ashes scattering in all directions.

    So he and Clifford
now lie here,
their days of drinking over.

    Drink must drown
the separateness of every "I"
so that ones "me" can join with others
in a camaraderie.
    Blaming persons doesn't help,
but perhaps more love
when we are sober
might be a start of something.

Not only have their days of drinking
gone to pasture
but, too, a way of farming life
moved by horses --
clip, clop, plodding, plodding, plodding.

   Old Rex --
sharp shouldered, straight necked, long nosed,
gray with specks of brown that glinted in his hide.
   Warts spurred the inner sides
of his ungainly legs.

   He won no beauty prize,
but he was smart,
and strong.
   In the stall or pasture,
he daydreamed as he flicked an ear,
wagged his lower lip, and rested up with one foot bent

and resting on its forward edge.
   No use wasting energy
or getting worked into a lather.

   His half closed eyes
held a pained expression
that sometimes burst afire,
but only in emergencies
that crashed into his working day.

   Sometimes when hitched with some unruly mate
he squealed his anger,
and bit the nearest part of the offending horse.
   Fooling wasted energy and snarled the harness.

   My dad named Rex --

(but he never called us by our names.
   He always called us "he" or "him" or "her",
and with sex identified
one usually knew the one he meant.

   Proper names embarrassed him;
and if in doubt one ventured "Who?",
in irritation he repeated "HIM!",
with emphasis!

   Perhaps he felt a primitive resistance
to objectify
and thus divide the whole,
for somehow naming
slices wholeness into pieces.

   It rubbed onto us,
and among ourselves we called him
"the old man",
and my mother, "the old lady".

   Who is my old man?

   These remains beneath this stone? --
this farm, this countryside? --

these neighbors past and present, my friends and family? --
the woods, the clearing, fields? --
the changing times? --
the roaring twenties, the depression, drought and war? --
the horses, cattle, sheep and dogs
that knew this place as home?

   I don't know.

   But its ridiculous
to think that he lies here.)

   At any rate
my dad named Rex
and taught him how to open gates
so that the driver needn't clamber off and on
his load.

   Rex learned his lesson well
and often let himself into the corn field or the oats.
   And, too, he bumped his head against the barn door
until the hook fell loose,
or rubbed his halter on his stall
until the strap slipped through the buckle.
   Then he roamed the barn,
ripped feed sacks open, strewed bran upon the floor,
and helped himself.

   We seldom caught him in the act;
he was always standing in his stall,
daydreaming in his innocence,
though droppings in the manger
and no halter on his head
identified the criminal.

   We grew up together,
Rex and I.

Now tractors do the work,
but one can't grow with them,
immediately they start to wearing out.
   One has a partnership with death,
not life and growth.
   Maybe this is why
with our machines
we find it difficult to be humane.
   To grow ourselves
we need to grow with other growing things.

   Rex
introduced me to the art of cultivating corn.
   First I rode him
up and down between the rows
while my dad would guide the cultivator.
   Then I drove him
with lines tied and looped around my neck
while I wrestled with the cultivator.

   Though exertion pained him,
yet Rex could snatch a nip of corn leaf in the passing
so quickly that I could not grab the lines
in time to stop the theft.

   To retaliate
I cussed him out.

   Swearing
I learned early
from my dad,
and others.

   He had reasons --
a mangled thumb,
a balking horse, a plugged up mower sickle,
and experience as a lumber jack.

   But I swore as a poetry of speech,
spiced with youthful vigor and imagination.
   I swore to prove my maleness
as my father's son.
   It put exclamations, asterisks and brackets
around my budding masculinity.

   Scandalized
my mother tried reform
that resulted mainly as restraint upon my dad.

I never heard a woman swear.

But Rex would nip a corn leaf,
munch his snack, flop his ears, and plod along
unmindful of the questions in his heritage
to which I called attention.

So with Rex's schooling
I became a teamster.

Endless wagon loads of peas
we rattled on this gravel road
past this quiet spot
on to the vinery down the road a bit.

It took skill
to bring a lurching wagon
through a rutted driveway
close beside the pitching chute.

I often shaved the chute by inches.
Once the foreman tried to get a piece of paper
in between the chute edge and the rack.
When my load approached
a signal brought the vinery men
to stand and watch the load lurch in --
and by.

It was too close for comfort,
but with my reputation

I had to sweat each load out through this crisis.
   I would have rather
pitched the vines a little further
but my honor was at stake.
   Had I yielded just an extra inch or two
I would have learned the art of compromise
a little sooner.

   I know the watchers hoped
that I would hit the chute,
and I would be the butt of some good-natured fun
with an undertone of malice.

   Luck smiled.

   Of course, old Rex
came on that inner side,
and I was never certain if it was my driving skill
or Rex's savvy.
   But I took the credit anyway,
and I do not notice others
letting credit dangle loose and unattached.

   At length
the vinery men were bragging of "their" driver.
   When it seemed more skill than luck,
they identified with me;
but had I hit the chute ----------!

   All that human ego,
theirs and mine,
built upon a single horse's sense.

Hauling gravel on the roads
involved a gang of shovelers
and half a dozen wagons.

   At the pit,
one carefully surveyed the ground
before he stopped the wagon
so that the team might easier get it started
once the shovelers filled the wagon box.

   The horses had a hard, dead pull
and a short, steep climb
out to the road above.

   When ready to move out,
one slowly tightened lines,
taut enough so that the horses
launched into the tugs together,
but loose enough to let them go.

   Unless they pulled together,
each pulled the other backward
and seesawed on the evener.

   Rex
never played that game of seesaw
but moved slowly to make sure that I was ready.
   He braced his legs,
took the shock of the other horse's launch,
then matched his strength and moved with him.

   Teamwork
moved that load of gravel
as inevitably as the sun
moves up and over the horizon.

   But today

leaders of the nations
don't seem to have one half the sense
old Rex displayed.

   Out of the pit,
heaving horses' rested.
   Strokings on the nose and neck
Rex accepted quite indifferently.
   He could do without plaudets;
his self-respect did not depend on recognition,
which is more than half
of growing up.

   Horses clopping on,
heads swinging rhythmically from side to side,
steel wagon tires grinding on the gravel road,
fine sand jiggling through the dump planks.

   Boredom.

   Glass cups

on telephone poles

paraded by.

   Here and there

bull's eye!

   Sometimes
one lazily threw a stone

with no intent to make a hit --
just a way to pass the time.

    Much destruction -- many injuries --
are unintentional,
just plain unthinking foolishness --
a way to puncture boredom.

    And many spirit wounds wouldn't cut so deep
if one would take the time
to find out if the injury were deliberate.
    For as the spirit goes,
intent makes all the difference.

    But as glass cups may go,
intent or no intent,
they shattered
on the impact.

    Rex teamed with many mates
that came and went.
    Old rat-tailed, faithful, willing Ned
teamed with him for awhile.

    Ned had been abused
before we got him.
    He jerked his head up high
at any sudden movement --
bridling, watering, or pitching hay.
    He often thumped his head
against the beams above his stall.
    He even jerked
the times I tried to pat his neck.

    Abuse
creates protective actions
behind which one retreats
when threatened.

    But friendliness
creates clear skies
in which one ventures out to sun himself.

I never got to Ned;
it made me sad;
I liked him.

Jack
turned out an outlaw.

He seemed sensible enough
when first we got him
and worked him every day.
But following a week or two of idleness
he'd act up --
charge back and forth,
rear up and shake his head --
throw front feet on the neck yoke,
or a hind leg over traces or the pole,
and get so hopelessly entangled in the harness
that straps he did not break
we had to cut
to get him out.

Sometimes my dad
tried to club him to obedience.
It never worked,
that was more of what had made him what he was.
There never seemed a reason,
just suddenly he went crazy.

Of course we club each other,
verbally or by spiteful actions.
Physically no wounds may show,
but deep within,
the spirit may be battered black and blue.
And then
such a one may do strange things,
and we call it mental illness.
But it is pretty certain
that such a person has a spirit
striped
with welts and wounds.

But clubbing never works;
Jack had to go.

   And Bess!

   One spring day
when muddy roads were rutted deep,
a neighbor stopped for help
to extricate his car
from the clutches of a sinkhole.

   Bess was the only horse at home that day,
and somewhat doubtfully I harnessed her
and led her to my friend's discouraged car.

   A burnished bay,
fourteen hundred pounds of muscled beauty,
black flowing tail and mane,
nervous, head held high, ears flickered back and forth
to catch the slightest sound.

   She chomped her bit,
shifted feet,
and turned her head
to glance back at this strange assignment
as I hooked the chain to car and whipple tree.

   Standing to one side,
I gently tightened lines.
   Fearful fire
flickered in her large black eyes.

   She trembled, poised, breath bated,

one ear cocked and one turned back.
   Then on a sharp "giddap"!
and flick of line that smartly clapped her rump,
she smacked into her collar,
body low, legs slanted straining,
chest bulging as to burst,
neck arching like a bended bow.

   For

      an

         eternity

the taut tugs

           agonized

                 between a balance

as the car roared helplessly

                         and spun its wheels.
"Pull, damn it, pull!"
A lump caught in my throat.

   Her body slowly tilted forward
like a boulder being pried from off a cliff.
   One flashing thumping step;
mud splattering in all directions.

   "Pull!"

   A sucking sound of front wheels
moving slowly in the mud.
   A gasping snort, another thumping step,
"We've got it going!" --
goose pimples skated up and down my back and neck --
a thump, a snort, a thump, a thump, a snort,
"Giddap! Giddap!"
   Straining, flashing, tensing muscles
blended into one enormous will and effort,
"Damn, keep it going!"

   A sudden jerk of chain --
the car slewed from side to side --
a quickening beat of hooves.
   I slipped and slid along the side
until the hind wheels of the car
lurched onto solid ground,
and spurting forward

ran up slack into the chain.

    "Whoa! Whoa! We did it!"

    Heaving, snorting, fidgeting from foot to foot,
she jerked her head up high
to glance upon this monster
she had rescued from the mud.

    "Whoa! That's it! Good girl!"
My voice seemed hoarse,
I trembled, things seemed misty.

    It took a tug upon the bit
to bend her head so I could stroke her nose,
rub her ear lobes, pat her neck.

    Unhitched,
she pranced and snorted,
as pulling on the lines,
she led the way on home.

    "Well, so long!"
I yelled back to my neighbor,
"Hope that crate will get you on to town."

    Though outwardly I wonder,
yet I know
why in later years
when I see some racing horses pounding to the finish line,
a lump constricts my throat,
goose pimples chase each other up and down my back,
and muffled sobs
oscillate within my chest.

Except for Mennonites,
tractors now provide horse power,
multiplying through the years
as horses dwindled
into feed for foxes
and for mink.

Richard Nordlund.

    He
always had a ready grin --
hearty salutations spiked with profanity --
ruddy, back slapping, hard drinking, worldly Dick.

    A bachelor lumberjack,
usually unemployed with the forests gone --
his skills less needed
as woods gave way to fields.
    He hid his lostness
behind a boisterous bravado and constant drinking.

    Drink got the best of him.

    My lumberjacking wasn't much --
just cutting firewood.

    Jigging axes at an angle
on a turning grindstone,
and sharpness tested with a thumb
drawn gingerly along the edge.

    A swinging, frosty
two mile hike
out to the woods.

    Ringing thwacks of axe on wood,
startled chips flew out in panic --
creak and woosh of falling trees --

chop and clip of limbing --
rhythmic swish, swish -- swish, swish --
of the two man crosscut saw;
struggling in deep snow to pile the logs and poles.

    Then later,
horses lurching breast high in snow
with an empty sleigh,
breaking roads about the cutting;
heaving logs and poles upon the heavy bunks
and chaining tight.

    Lunging horses
break the runners loose.
    Once moving,
sleighs run easily,
especially in an icy rut.

    But breeching with the martingales attached
equip resisting horses with a brake
upon a downhill stretch;
or a loaded sleigh will slide upon them,
the sleigh pole pushing neck yokes and the collars
high up on their necks;
and once going,
either horses must outrun the sliding sleigh
or get run over
with the sleigh and log load piling up.

    Sliding down an endless icy slope
with ineffective brakes and maximums,
our society can't slow down either
and we've got to run or get run over.

    A few days hauling
and the pile of poles increased
into a small sized mountain
in the yard at home.

    Then,
hum of circle saw,
lugging logs and poles
shoved rumbling on the bench
up to the bumper for each cut,
pushing tabled poles into the screaming saw,
throwing blocks --
sodden mittens, trousers torn, aching backs.

With ears still ringing,
respite in the house --
hot coffee, meat, potatoes, gravy, pie
and satisfaction --
for that day at least.

Leon Nahring --

born more than 100 years ago --

wood butcher for the logging camps.

With axe and saw
he carved the neck yokes,
whipple trees, and sleigh bunks
and a host of other wooden things
to keep the camps in operation.

Though he butchered wood
he didn't care to butcher animals,
and he often called upon my dad
to do his butchering,
maybe for the way in which my dad would do it
as much as for his skill.

Once my dad left a knot shaped piece of bright green s[o]
smack in the middle of the dark turned soil
of his spring plowing.
He never told us,
but then when we investigated,
we found a killdeer's nest.

Sometimes I held a heifer by the halter
while my dad would grip a heavy hammer in one hand,
and with the other
gently stroke her forehead
to find the spot
for an instant coup de grace.

    Time

        strolled

              by.

Was he showing his affection for the animal,
or mustering resolve?

As signal that the moment had arrived,
he glanced at me,
slowly swung the hammer back
and with a single blow,
dropped the heifer in a heap upon the ground,
and quickly cut its throat.

The physical dismantling
came later.

What said, "Now!",
a readiness of his emotions
or a rational decision?

What really
sorts our future out?

Pigs
won't stand so docilely
before the hammer.

One time our neighbor
used his twenty-two to help us.
To shoo away some doubt,
he enthused about his special cartridges.

"Crack!"

Instead of dropping,
the pig ran zig zag,
squealing bloody murder,
all around the pen.

Then it stopped a moment,
head down, grunting.

"Crack!"

With an uproarious squealing,
it scrambled back and forth,
crashing into boards and wire,
stumbling over troughs and stones.

Its hellish squealing
pierced one to the core of being.
My mother almost had a fit,
running in and out the house,
yelling in distress
to put that tortured animal
out of its misery.

The shells were nearly gone
before it fell.

No twenty-two again!

Life feeds on life,
and even vegetarians
destroy the living embryos in flour
or the living cells in salad greens.

No escaping that.

But ones conscience may protest
the killing of a pig
as a demonstration
of the special merits of one's cartridges or gun,
and shake ones aim.

Buying

meat
removes one from the living confrontation,
and one only worries for his money's worth.

   The way a thing is done
is all important --

even

      sin.

   Semiannually
the cattle buyer stopped
to see my dad.

   The weather judged
and found wanting.

   "Say, Carl,
any cows you want to sell?"

   "O o o o o oh,
this just freshened heifer,
maybe."

   "How much?"

   "Two hundred."

"Well, Carl,
I don't know.
   One twenty,
perhaps......

you belong to that tractor
out in front?"

   "Yup."

Its pros and cons
raked over.

   "Would you take one forty for her?"

   "W e e e e ell,
she's one of my best young cows --
one eighty
at the very least."

   Politics reviewed.

   "If you really want her
I'll let her go
for one hundred seventy."

   "No. Really.
one fifty
is the best that I can do."

   Stories swapped.

   "Ha - ha - ha - a - a. Ya.
   That's really good.
   Well, before I go,
I'll up it to
one fifty-five."

"Can't give her to you.
   One sixty-five,
rock bottom."

   "Say,
hear that Bob Swenson
lost his leg?
   Tree slipped back from off the stump
and pinned him."

   Logging incidents recalled.

   "Well, got to be going.
   Tell you what,
split the difference."

   "One sixty,
even?"

   "One sixty."

   "She's worth more,
but,
guess I could use the money."

   "Fine,
I'll send a truck tomorrow."

   So went half the morning.

   Once our cat
had kittens in the manger in the barn.

One morning I came charging out
full of anticipated furry cuddling
to see a strange tom cat
go skatting out the open barn door --
and then the kittens --
bloody, mangled, strewn dead upon the hay.

"You son-of-a-bitch!",
I screamed, raging at the cat
receding fast across the field.

"You bastard!"

Then kneeling down
and stroking bloody fur,
I whimpered half aloud,
"The goddam son-of-a-bitch!"

I hate tom cats
no matter who they are.

Old Leon's driveway,
there just across the road,
tells quite a tale.

Flames
leapt from a wooden cross
that someone planted in our driveway
one night.

The Klu Klux Klan, we thought --
a warning,
or an invitation to my dad to join.

The charred remains
revealed an expert's handiwork.

Kids at school
told tales of how the Catholics
burned some little kids in ovens.

I didn't know what a Catholic was;
but now I do,
and also now I know
from where those tales most likely came.

The burning of that cross
was lost on me --
except for an idea.

Next day, up in the haymow,
I nailed two boards together cross ways,
wrapped them round with rags
and soaked them well with kerosene.

That night
we sneaked up through the pasture
to old Leon's driveway
set it up and lit it.

    Flames
seared the night;
but lights
within that house
went out.

    Fear.

    In daylight
the charred uneven boards and battered nails
showed the work of kids;
and for some reason
fingers seemed to point in my direction.

    It was all in fun;
we didn't know that they'd be frightened half to death.
    That's the way with kids;
they don't see beyond their noses,
as my mother used to say.

    But the story
took the wind
out of cross burnings by the Klan.
    Maybe that's the way
to deal with hate and prejudice --
show it for the joke it is,
though it isn't funny.

An early pioneer about these parts,
Frank Moore.

   All I remember is a handlebar moustache
that steered his face
as he drove a tractor --
poomp, poomp, poomp --
down the road.

   Poomp, poomp, poomp
like the huff, huff, huff
of a steam engine
powering a threshing machine.

   Threshing --

     Threshing
meant a gang of men --
field pitchers,
lofting bundles with a pitchfork
up and up upon the wagon;
wagon drivers,
frantically arranging order on the load
amid a pummeling of bundles sailing in from every side,
some aimed with disconcerting accuracy;
spike pitchers
forking bundles from the wagon
to the apron feeding gnashing knives;

machine operators,
adjusting, oiling, standing there on top
as though some kind of king;
grain sack carriers,
hoisting sacks of a hundred pounds or so
to the shoulder
and lurching toward the grain bin;
sack tender,
one who tended grainsacks as they filled
and tied them --
an honorary job for older men.

Threshing meant a gang of men --
men and boys, that is --
and, counting kitchen help,
women folk, including girls.

Boys of twelve
just old enough to drive a team of horses
through to men near seventy or more
toiled and joked together.

"That youngster sure can take it!"

"Boy, I hope I've got some spunk like that
when I'm that old."

Steam engines added drama
to an already main event --
a huffing, puffing iron monster
spinning pulleys and a governor,
belching smoke, squirting steam,
while angry flames leered and leapt
through cracks within the fire box.

A flashing piston drove the pulley on the belt

that ran the thresher --
another monster
spinning pulleys, belts,
and flashing knives that slashed and cut,
voraciously devouring bundles that the spiker fed it.
    All disappeared into its jiggling digestive system;
then it gently sifted kernels into sacks;
but, gorged beyond retention,
it spewed the straw from out the blower to the stack,
chaff swirling all around,
and sifting down the wind like golden snow.

    But all that now is gone,
for now a single man upon a combine
can do the job alone --
alone and lonely.

    In a community
we have need of one another.
    But with modern day technology
we can do things easier,
eat much more for smaller costs,
own more things,
underwrite a spanking new abode in some suburbia,
for the secondary price of

        loneliness.

    With a consumer attitude,
we live to eat;
but with a qualitative attitude,
we eat to live.

    And, oh, the meals
the women served to threshing crews.
    Mounds of everything --
meat, potatoes, gravy, salads, bread,
topped off with pie and cake;
and pervading all,
a spirit full of jest and banter,

and on the side
flirtation with the girls who waited on the tables.

    Haying --
just a family operation.

    A wave of startled grass tops,
just above the moving sickle bar,
staggered and fell back in swathes.

    A spiteful side delivery rake
kicked the curing hay
in windrows.

    The maternal loader,
hitched behind the wagon,
picking up the windrowed hay,
but never stopping for an Angelus.

    Shiny tines of pitchforks
swirled the offerings of the loader
forward on the rack.

    Cascades of leaves and chaff
showered on the head and down the neck
of the teamster.

    Plodding horses --
swinging, sweating, lathered foamy white
along the harness straps rubbing on their backs and rumps,
and flecked with hay and chaff.
    Creaking hames on collars,
croaking wheels and groaning rack.

    "Hit those furrows at right angles, stupid!
Wanta tip us over?"

    Well, it wouldn't be the first time.

At the barn,
jumping on the hay fork,
urging it to take a deeper bite into the load.

   "Go 'head!"

   Hustling horses
pulling on the hay rope
riding through protesting pulleys.

   Click! Zoom!
   The hay fork load swung in along the track,
trailing skirts and petticoats.

   With the trip -- "Come back!"

   Smaller fry
struggling slack up on the hay rope.

   In the mow,
hay heaved to either side
from underneath the track.

   With the haying season's end,
heaping dishesful of ice cream
melting cool within ones mouth
and down the throat.

   But this now too is past
with other means of haying taking over.
   It's faster, easier, cleaner work;
and yet I'm glad that I participated
in the drama of those harder, less efficient times,
though I wouldn't now repeat them.

   Yes,
the drama now has lessened --
the people versus elements.

Only two years old.

    I missed a day of school to be his pallbearer --
a winter cutter ride;
at their house,
casual conversation walked on stilts
and halfhearted jokes hung suspended in the air;
a minister's solemn intonations;
a sleigh ride back to here
where I helped to carry him.

    As a boy eleven years,
here I stood by ruddy frozen earth
heaped up beside an oblong hole
gaping in the snow.

    Reality glared open eyed --
no modern velvet treatment --
and no one thought I was too young.

    Friends and neighbors
dug all these other graves.

    Death
seems more acceptable
with a shovel in ones hands.

    It was cold that day --
the middle of the winter.

    On freezing days,
so cold that snow creaked under foot,
one moved within a fairyland of crystals.

    Frost,
suspended in the air
like feathery flakes that lightly turned and twisted,
glinted prism colors
while twin rainbows ringed the sun.

Hunched shoulders
tightened up the collar round my neck
and sealed my body warmth within,
even as the spirit draws together
to muster its resources.

Whitened puffs of breath
streamed past my face,
frosting eyebrows, cheeks, and earflap cap.

One moved enchanted
in a sparkling, glinting, glistening,
rainbow-crystalled fairyland.

When glistening sheets of ice
glazed the fields,
at night,
a silvery pathway gleamed for half a mile or more
on to the rising moon.

Tan tips of grass
and tops of weeds
neck deep in snow --
brown seeds scattered on the white expanse --
snow buntings pecking, flitting, chipping.

Tropic ferns
and fronds of palms
etched in frost upon the window panes.

With central heating
frost no longer spangles windows.
One sees through them,
which is what they're for,

I guess.

Skating on the pond at night --
gliding, floating, turning --
like a man in space,
and darkness pressing soft and gently
close on every hand.

Running over snow encrusted roads at night
for fun --
woodlots, whitened meadows, lighted windows drifting by --

and stars --

stars that seemed to leap and sing
in glittering prismatic fire.

Hanging to a rope tied to a car,
arching wide on skis into the fields,
and at the latest moment possible
swinging back into the road
to miss a tree, or rock, or fence.

Sometimes, too late,
one had to let the rope go free
and with frantic scarecrow antics
upend into the snow to stop in time.

Dropouts know what they're about.

Snow and storm;
marooned in town.

Hiking home next morning
through a foot or more of drifted snow.

A frosted orange sun
just rising on the white horizon.

A railroad engine
huffed and puffed just out of town
sending mushroom clouds of smoke and steam
billowing high and white
into the frosty morning air.

The beauty of this sight
has bowed its head
and passed into oblivion with steam engines.
And too that white and billowing mushroom cloud
no longer makes the heart strings sing
but beats the drums of fear.

Can it be
that man's intent,
like colored glasses,
tints the world with beauty
or with ugliness?

Beauty must be cherished
where and when it's found;
it's rare because it doesn't last;
beauty doesn't stop
to be ones guest,
but rather one must stop for it
and be its guest.

Silence
speaks of secrets
in the snowbound woods.

Swish and thump of skis;
snow edged twigs of birch and maple
peered out and floated by.
Pine and hemlock needles
smirked beneath snow laden limbs.
Spruce pagodas
brooded in the stillness,
and balsams
drooped in snowy meditation.

Breath wafted slowly upward.

Hooh, hooh, hooh who-o-o-o!

An owl voiced an exclamation point
to the silence.

Having felt a pulse of life,

shared a mood of mystery,

sensed a silent laughter,

I turned about to slide along my ski trail;
hurrying in the dusk
so that darkness did not catch me
still within the woods.

   Had I worshipped?

   No.
   I think one worships from the outside;
rather, I had been with being.

   Soon a lightening of the dusk
marked the edge of woods,
and there beyond the fields
buildings slid in view,
black blocks upon a white expanse,
our house marked out by yellow lights from windows.

   After evening chores out in the barn,
the family sat around the Franklin stove,
glowering red hot spots upon its belly.
   We read,

played checkers, cards, or carrom,
or just drowsed before the heat.
   One brother
often fell asleep upon the floor
between the wall and stove.

   We slept upstairs,
and an open attic yawned,
dark and threatening,
up above the stairway.
   When one
decided it was time for bed,
all
of us bolted up the stairs,
shouldered through the doorway,
slammed the bedroom door behind us,
and dived into our beds --
two in one,
three in another.

   Though we sensed each other's fears,
each kept it secret.

   Or was I the only one?

   I didn't notice
any dallying of the others.

   No monster spirits plagued my mind,
no leering devils,
and yet that vague uneasiness.
   We knew that nothing occupied the attic
for we played up there --

in daylight.

   And in the morning,
though darkness lingered,
the fear had fled.

   Did our relatives in trees
fear a predator that stalked
as soon as darkness fell?

   Who conjured up

the gargoyles on Notre Dame?
   Who made hell a place of darkness
and heaven a place of light?
   Who invented devils,
imps, chimera, vampires, ghosts?

   I know who,

but

I'm not saying.

   As snow drifts melted down
and grass began to green,
the joy of running
flung shoes from off the feet.

   Mud and meadow muffins
squirmed satisfyingly
up between the toes,
like noodle ribbons.

   In dry weather,
thick dust on roads
felt soft and cool upon the feet,
fine lines and wrinkles
showing in the imprints.

   Bare feet had its price
of punctures and stubbed toes
and washing when to bed.

   A neighbor kid and I,
bare headed,

in ragged shirts
and torn and faded overalls,
strolled barefooted on a dusty road,
recounting all the riches
that our parents had amassed.

Then I didn't know
that wealth is not possessions
but just ones state of mind,
a sense of needs fulfilled.

And yet now that I know,
still my possessions
wreck my wealth.

In fall
before the sun was up,
I often ran through frosted grass
to get the cows for milking,
lingering where a cow had lain
to warm my feet.

In the winter
bare feet often tested snow and ice,
usually on a dare.

Yes,
"How beautiful
are thy
feet
upon the hills."

With winter past
came spring
and the return of birds.

   Crows,
the Paul Reveres in March
flying northward cawing out the imminence of spring,
in June were Recoats camouflaged in black
laying taxes on our newly planted corn.

   Wrens,
scolding everyone on general principles.

   Bob-o-links,
bubbling song while on the wing
and sinking in a field of grass
with a tail-end, "spink, spank, spink".

   Robins,
building up morale
with cheerios and cheeriups.

   English sparrows,
socializing at their church bazaars.

   Purple martins,
soaring, sailing, gurgling.

   Killdeers,
calling frantically,
luring one away
from their spindle-legged, fuzzy, dime sized young
that looked like milkweed down

blowing whimsically before the wind.

    Yellow breasted meadowlarks,
the proper middle class about the fields.

    The screech owl,
housewifely standing in her knothole,
blinking, staring, ruffling feathers
as she rubbernecked.

    Kingbirds,
medieval knights of airways,
driving crows and hawks away
with acrobatic swoops and dives upon their heads.

    Sparrow hawks,
making sudden swoops
at sparrows in the barn.

    Flickers,
the Romeos and Juliets of woodland birds,
sporting polka dotted yellow vests
and black bowties.

    Eave swallows,
with family gatherings on telephone lines,
waiting for their bedtime story.

    Blue birds,
colorful,
but law-abiding residents.

    Chimney swifts,
veering high aloft,
the gallant young men on the aerial trapeze.

    Chipping sparrows,
incessantly insistent.

    Shrikes,
the scourge of fields and woods,

impaling mice and smaller birds on thorns.

The Gerings.

   Wind whipped whistling
through my jacket, cap and woolen mittens
on the way to school one winter morning.
   Gasping, crying, tingling cold,
I stopped at Olive's house.

   She rubbed my whitened hand with snow
until the threatened frostbite disappeared.
   Then later,
warmed and bundled up,
she sent me on back home
helped by blustering wind behind me.

   But George
seemed somewhat truculent,
though perhaps he didn't mean to be.

   Somehow he invited challenge,
and we plotted all year long
the tricks we'd do
when under cover of the night on Halloween --
like rattling ticktacks on his window panes,
soaping windows, tipping privies,
pulling wagons, hay rakes, mowers
off into the fields or high up on a stone pile,
unrolling rolls of wire,
harnessing the bull,
dismantling some machine or vehicle
and reassembling on a shed roof or the barn,
piling logs and stumps in driveways --

   George's dander

always fused excitement.
   One Halloween
our gang had run his wagon off
with too much telltale noise;
and stealing back,
a faintly squeaking screen door
opening and closing
halted us,
and in the dark
we strained our ears.

   "Blam!"

   A shotgun blast
sent us scurrying round the barn,
through the fence,
and on into the pasture.

   There we lay behind a knoll
to reconnoitre our retreat
and reorganize our strategy.
   But soon a dusky figure
moved along the barn wall,
stopping at the corner nearest us.

   One of our pranksters panicked
and hoarsely whispered that George had seen us
and might shoot
so loud we thought that he had given us away.
   We held him down
and shut him up.

   Our hearts were thumping in our ears
as two eternities

                   dawdled

                        by

before he slowly moved the way he came;

then we took off.

No further tricks that night,
there at least.

In school next day,
we plotted what we'd do next year.

Today,
when children ring the bell
and ask me for a "trick or treat",
and if I say, "let's have a trick!",
they stand with mouths agape.

How can they know?

We might call their candy plunder,
but rather it's the pay off in a bribe.

George
would have felt let down
had we solicited a treat
for good behaviour.

He respected us,
and we respected him --

and his gun.

So now they both lie here.

I'm sure that Olive must have cautioned George
to be careful with that gun

and waited anxiously
for him to come back in.

		Up there on the bridge,
Oscar, here,
often spouted off
and gave us hell
for swimming in the raw.

	We shed our clothes
too slowly as it was
in bushes swarming with mosquitoes
without adding time for bathing suits.

	Besides,
if the need arose,
we could cup a hand
to shield our dignity
in transit to the river.

	I never understood
if our private parts
possessed the awesome dignity of deity
that should be shielded from the common gaze
or the damnation of the devil.

But only boys were swimming,
and
he didn't own the river.

He called us pigs.

But no pigs I've seen
like their mud that thin --
you see
Black River
earns its name.

Old Jim Leonard.

His glassed in Model T
passed our place
on his occasional trip to town.

A bachelor,
his farm, machinery, buildings
and his car
all became a wife to him --
deserving tender care.

Model Ts
had no speedometers;
but one could speed along so recklessly
that fence posts crowded by
too fast for counting.

That was going some.

The Hudson Super Six
roared past them all --

though I never saw one.

My old man
bought a second hand Model T Ford pickup
for me to drive to school with;
and just incidentally,
my passengers included cream cans
destined for the creamery,
and feed sacks full of oats
that needed grinding at the feed mill.

When we got it,
I drove it home alone
and my dad followed in the other car.

The salesman told me
after he had cranked it up,
"Steer with this wheel;
this lever regulates the speed;
now to get her going
push your foot down on this pedal --
go ahead and do it."

Then from the running board,
"To get her into high,
just let it out."

My instructor jumped,
and somewhat to my consternation,
I was on my way.

Eight miles later
I weaved into our driveway,
and then panicked
on how to stop the thing.

They must have phoned out to my mother
that Pegasus would soon arrive
and needed briefing on a way to stop.
She was outside yelling something --
all I heard was "push",
and I already had all three pedals
pushed as far as they would go,
hoping maybe one was right.

At least I missed the barn and chickhouse
and headed out into the field beyond,
and then the car choked dead and stopped
with fifty feet of fencing trailing in my wake.

My driver's education
cost that fifty feet of fence,
which wasn't much
for a lesson blazoned on my soul
by scaring half the living daylights out of me.

We never owned a Model A.

When they came out
and nearly everybody sported one
my dad
goaded envy with an Essex,
and then a Nash.

A blunted plowshare
thrown into the car
meant stopping at the blacksmith's shop.

The smith would wedge the share
in smouldering coals upon his forge.

Sweeping strokes upon the bellows
blew the coals white hot,
and soon the share grew red
then white with heat.

With the moment right,
he grasped the share with tongs,
withdrew it from the coals,
and placed it on the anvil.

A few reflective taps
with his hammer on the anvil
rang out like a bell.
Then with measured blows
his hammer thudded on the white hot iron,
bursting sparks in all directions.

Sweat beaded his Herculean frame
bare to the waist.

Muscles tensed and glided
underneath his glistening
dirt streaked skin.
Breath wooshed out with every stroke,
while the share began to grow a pointed tip

and sharper edge
under muffled thudding;
but as the iron cooled a darker red,
it began to ring in protest.

    Then again upon the forge
to heat once more.

    Creation seems to have its time,
and the creator must know when to ply his trade.

    By golly,

I can see our old school
a whole mile west of here.

    Things have changed --
trees are gone --

the view extended wider, farther.

School --

eight grades, one teacher, and one room --

I could have done without.

What I remember most
went on outside --
like playing ball
with any number but the regulation nine.

We never lost a game --
when the score implied it,
the other side had either cheated
or the ump was blind or watching girls.

And when recruits were scarce
we played without an ump;
both teams disputed
any play within a ten foot error margin --
whether running bases or the strike zone.

After threats of mass assault and battery,
or to quit,
play resumed with cries of
"Cheaters", "Cry babies", "O, let'm have it",
reverberating from each side.

Good sportsmanship?

I wonder if it's only training
in accepting 2nd place, or 3rd, or 4th --
conditioning for eventual inequality --
represented by the score,
or by ones income.

Only losers
need to be good sports.

But no one lost
in our games.

Everybody won;
either by the score
or by forfeit due to serious default
in the other team's integrity.

Pum pum pullaway;
come or we'll pull ya way;
ante, ante over;
rough and tumble; monkey pile;
winter downhill sliding
on our sawmill slabs,
or the richer kids
on skis.

Teachers reigned
by force of different means.

One used a heavy ruler
that she walloped across ones palm.
   It really stung,
and the bigger kids got it on the knuckles.

Another kept you after school or in at recess;
others made you work -- sweep floors or dust erasers;
one pulled ears and hair;
another flexed a strap
across ones hinder in the coat room.

    Once
the teacher summoned me
for encounter with that strap of leather.
    My unusually long sweater
veiled the target,
and with every wallop,
enveloped the strap
and clung
so that the belting didn't even touch me.

    Though rendered ineffectual
by flailing on my sweater tail,
and by stifled laughter,
the teacher made her point,
with no injury to me.

    A certain honesty infused it all.

    We were being trained
and made to do what we were told
because adults were bigger.

    Now it's gilded over
with student government, questionnaires,
elective subjects, understanding, counselling,
good citizenship awards --
but still a student does as he is told
because adults are bigger.

    Yes, I know;
I'm still playing at a baseball game
that I cannot afford to lose.

With women teachers,
the boy's outhouse
commanded sanctuary,
within whose holy walls
no one but males might tread.

At times
when clouds of smoke reaked through the cracks,
it seemed the place must be on fire,
for there we smoked contraptions
made of tobacco snitched from someone's dad
and rolled in torn squares of paper.

When someone couldn't steal the he-man's article,
we smuggled in a pocket full of chaff and hayseed.

Our creations looked like knotty bludgeons,
or at best, odd shaped cigars;
and in the course of fervent puffing,
or putting out an open flame,
burning contents tumbled down one's front
and on the floor.

Smoke became so thick
one didn't need a cigarette.

But **we** were safe,
we budding men,
from teacher intervention.

Outhouse immunity
lured one kid
to bootleg in a pint of moonshine.

Each clamoured for his turn

to scorch his throat
with liquid fire
that flamed surprise in eyes as well;
and then,
through coughing,
choking, stammering, and burning tears,
exclaimed upon its merit.

   Rumour tattletaled
that this kid's dad
was making it.

   He didn't come to school
for a few days after that
and when he did,
he took his seat quite gingerly.

   Fritz Kramer.

He grinned from ear to ear
despite hard times
and an ailing constitution.

He was the last
to run a small cheese factory.

I loitered there
from childhood through some three proprieters --
firing up the boiler,
sampling freshly salted curds --
and watched them
slicing up a vat of thickened milk --
stirring, draining whey,
pressing, boxing,
finally dipping long horn cheeses
in a vat of paraffin.

A one man operation.

No cause to mourn
that now enormous factories,
more efficient,
make the cheeses that a hundred smaller ones
made before.

No cause to mourn
these casualties of progress --

just so we know
that though the price of cheese
may be relatively lower than before,
it costs as much

or more.

Two brothers

killed in an accident --

one home on leave.

So young.

Like my sister,

who was just nineteen --

    At some thirty miles an hour,
something distracted her,
and the car swerved toward the ditch.
    On refocusing,
she swung the wheel away too hard;
the car rolled over once,
and up upon its wheels again.

    When I got out,
she was getting up from off the road.

    Her door had buckled open;
she fell out;
and the car rolled over her.

    She asked if anyone was hurt,
and then collapsed.

    A farmer took her on in to the hospital.

    No one else was hurt
of the **five** of us,
except for scratches;
and I drove the car on home,
and told the folks.

    They went right in.

While we boys were milking,
they phoned the neighbors;
and one came down
to tell us she had died.

   A confusion of emotions
choked out response;
what could we do
but keep on milking,

squirting milk

            by hand

                  into a pail --

   When they
inquired for a plot,
some pious soul behind the scenes
commented
that my folks remembered where the church was

only at such times as that --

so, due to offended feelings
she is buried elsewhere
though she had given much,
teaching Sunday school
and producing Christmas programs,
for this church.

Our neighbors across the road from us
found another resting place as well.

Rosie --

it matched her disposition.

Crippled with arthritis
in her later years
still her laugh and smile broke through.

Their boy and I
hit if off quite well.

We wrestled on the lawn long after dark --
laughing, giggling, grunting.

He taught me how to trap,
or perhaps we learned the art together.

Once
beside a stone pile on an edge of field
I found a hole.

Fresh earth,
the pungent smell of musk,
telltale hairs,
spelled skunk.

Visions of Canadian trappers,
of prices in the Hudson Bay Fur Company's catalogue,
of sudden wealth
leapt through my mind.

The trap was sprung,
a time or two
but then one day I made my catch.

Black
with two white stripes along its back,
my victim struggled with its foot gripped by the trap
anchored to a heavy root.

Success! Prestige!
Glory! Dollar signs!

After savouring my good fortune for a while,
I slowly realized the skunk was very much alive.
　　To have its pelt
I had to kill it.

　　I found a heavy stick,
and as I stalked
the skunk turned round and raised its tail.

　　Stand-off.

　　What to do --
that club was pretty much bravado anyway.
　　But there that skunk confronted me --
hugging close the ground,
and tugging on its foot.

　　Confusion --
conflicting thoughts
swept in scalding and in icy waves
through my consciousness.

　　Well,
I would let it go!
　　This one
anyway.

　　In the euphoria of that solution
I started forward,
but scudded to a stop
when that tail again raised high.

　　How do we communicate
after catching something in a trap?

　　And once involved,
how does one disengage?

　　With spirit chastened
I went back home to get the twenty-two.

　　On returning,
I found the trap jaws only clutched
a bunch of hairs.

"The lucky beggar",
I muttered to myself.

Weasel
hunted mice
in clumps of dry and brittle grass
along the creek,
or in a stump or brushpile,
and left successive colons
punctuated in the snow.

One spiked a piece of meat onto a stick
so that it hung enticingly
just above the pan.

If one caught a weasel,
it was dead and frozen stiff
when one arrived.

I suppose
it's something like long distance shooting
or bombing from the air.
It's all so far away

ones emotions cannot get involved.

    One isn't really present
at the coup de grace.

    And even executioners
feel faceless underneath their hoods.

    For rabbits
one made a snare from picture wire
and strung it from a stick
one placed across a runway.

    When a rabbit ran its head into the loop.
he pulled it tight,
and strangled through his struggles.

    Only once I had a confrontation.

    A cottontail
leapt frantically in all directions.

    With every leap
the snare snapped taut about its neck
and jerked it down from out the air,
while the stick would flip
and thrash the snow.

    Sickened
by that panicked struggle,
I turned and went back home.

Next morning

cold and quiet reigned.

I pulled a stiffened cottontail
from beneath a lacy spread of newly fallen snow --
almost sufficient to obliterate
the pellets of its dung
and the yellow stain of urine.

A rabbit
brought a quarter from a neighbor.

Oh,
he could have snared them too,
but didn't.

Many of us carnivores
would be vegetarians overnight
if we had to kill our meat.

I know now
of one
for certain.

But if the devil leers
from the visage of a victim,
killing comes much easier.

Woodchucks
maliciously dug their burrows in the fields.
Animals might break a leg by stepping in them --

though they never did --
or in heavy grass,
the mower sickle often ran into their piles of dirt
that plugged it up
and skid the drive wheel.

   So,
we filled up milk cans full of water,
and hauled them in the car
up to a freshly excavated hole.

   While we poured the water in,
Gyp and Patchy
whined and dug sporadically.

   The muddy water finally stirred
and a ratish looking head poked up.
   The two dogs snatched him
in the twinkling of an eye,
shaking him by turns,
and then each tugging on an end
tore him right in two.

   They had no need for our demonic yelling
urging them to make the kill;
and with our waving arms and jumping all about
adding to the pandemonium,
it seemed that we were celebrating
some macabre dance of death.

   Woodchucks now are scarce,
and I have added to their near demise.

   Whatever human senselessness
led to extinction of great auks
and of the carrier pigeons
seems to have some ground in me.

   How can conflict be creative?

   That's the poser.

I doubt that a passivity
will smile away our latent violence.

　　　Like
celebration of the Fourth.

　　　It burst out two weeks before,
then spluttered for another week beyond.

　　　Fire crackers
came in an array of sizes, shapes, and bangs.

　　　Thrown in the air
they cracked the loudest;
but also they exploded craters in the ground,
erupted heaps of dust into the air,
blew tin cans sky high,
shot out of bottles.

　　　And too,
one placed some carbide in a can,
added water,
tightly forced the cover on,
laid it on its side -- held down with a foot --
held a finger on a nail hole in the bottom,
and in some seconds after fumes had generated,
held a match up to the hole.

　　　The explosion
blew the cover off and sailing,
like a canon.

　　　Nighttime lighted up with sizzlers,
rockets, and with cherry bombs.

　　　On the morning of the Fourth,

older boys blasted dynamite.

    Today,
for safety's sake,
fireworks are prohibited,
except for those displays
by adults
which are carefully controlled;
and one becomes a spectator
rather than participant.

    Good reason for the change,
but participation
always carries risk.

    Freedom
means the future's unpredictable.

    But in a safe society
run by experts,
we become spectators
at the show
that we're supposed to be the actors in.

So be it.

The now

moves on

and

I must go

with a certain sense of loss

in me

or in the times.

I tell myself

each generation has its beauty

and its ugliness;

but looking back

it's mostly beauty.

The here and now

still blows reveille for me

upon its bugle.

Today

has business

to which I must attend.

So,

I'll leave the old man here,

          and

               get

                    going ---------

www.ingramcontent.com/pod-product-compliance
Lightning Source LLC
Chambersburg PA
CBHW060417090426
42734CB00011B/2342